Sit Down And Have A Beer Again

Greg Wyss

Cholla Needles Arts And Literary Library
Joshua Tree, California

Acknowledgements:

Part 1
Sit Down And Have A Beer was published in 1977 by Realities Library in San Diego, California. Poems & stories in the chapbook were first published by Duck Down Press, Images, Next, Moon Publications, Mudborn Press, Vagabond, The Fault, Roundtable Magazine, and Seven Stars Poetry.

Part 2
Poems and stories were first published by Duck Down Press, Vega Magazine, Seven Stars Poetry, Circus Maximus, Third Eye Magazine, Nitty-Gritty Magazine, Yearbook of Modern Poetry, and The Village Idiot.

Part 3
Story and dream sequences originally appeared in the novel *When Life Was Like A Cucumber*, Page Publishing.

DEDICATION

For anyone who lived through the 70's and can
pretend to remember them clearly
and
Those who have been born since and want to learn
how to avoid repeating this history

*"Those who cannot remember the past
are condemned to repeat it"*

-George Santayana

CONTENTS

Sit Down And Have A Beer   3

Even More Beer Pleasures   55

Final Taste of the 1970's   139

INTRODUCTION

The poems and stories that make up *Sit Down and Have A Beer*, the first chapter here, were in a chapbook published in 1977 by Realities Library. The stories and poems had been published in small press magazines impacting a small cadre of creatives in the country in those days.

The Small Press world of those days was the precursor to the internet – insane editors and publishers who believed that the established publications had simply lost touch with the creative reality of our nation. And, just like the internet, the small presses were eventually bought out by the rich folks who figured out the best way to beat them was to buy them out.

The second chapter of the book contains the other poems that were published in these mags but never collected till now.

The third chapter represents a small sample from *When Life Was Like A Cucumber*, the great novel about the early 1970's that tells the story of a young man's journey of self-discovery and sexual awakening as he tries to find his place in post-Sixties America.

SIT DOWN AND HAVE A BEER

SIT DOWN, HAVE A BEER

sit down, have a beer
the world has lost
its mind
anyway

don't give it
a second thought
pour down the novocain
buy your buddy one too
he aint got it
any better than you

get plastered
outa your mind
& when the place
closes for the night
make sure
you're out cold
make them drag you out
it's the least
they can do
for you

A TALE OF TWO GARBAGE MEN

i called them to come out
& pick up the garbage
they had forgotten
the day before
they said there'd be
an extra charge of $5
& when they got here
they still weren't going
to take it all

hey, fellas, I said
do you think you could
take all of it this time
i mean, it would be dumb
to have to come out here again
wouldn't it?

well, they went into
this big conference
whispering & all the time
eyeing me suspiciously
i began to wonder
if i had just made
an unreasonable request
but these guys
had a streak of good
running thru them
sure, they said &
then made ME load
the shit on the truck

i loaded it
thanked the bastards
went back inside
& rolled some shit
to smoke

DREAM

Outside the rain has begun to fall
darkness fills the study and the hall
as I pick up my hat and
waving everybody a good night
start disappearing in the foliage
never noticing the heavy footsteps
breathing erotically
in the autumn forests
go breathe on someone else's neck
i proclaim as i march forth
dreaming of gentle ice cream mountains
where life is a beggar's paradise
                    lost
forever
   in the pits
      of lovestained heartaches
like butter dripping thru the floorboards
on the bald heads of cigar smoking eunuchs
who completely undisturbed keep polishing their
toenails
for Saturday's parade
and as always
mama is watching
thru bluestained windows
invisible to their subjective eyes
the sun vanishes
and everywhere is silence...
and yesterday becomes a cave
concealing treasures mounted on tombs
of unknown soldiers?

THE COAST IS CLEAR

yeh, you've dug yourself
a big hole
a foxhole
like you've seen
in an old ww2 flick
i don't blame you
i'd hide too
but listen up
i've been checking out
your situation &
the way i see it
you can come out
now
the president has left
the generals have left
the armies have left
the boss has left
the wife has left
the kids have left
the car payments have left
the tv has left
the con men have left
even your dog
has wandered off somewhere
it's ok
you can come out
now
the coast is clear

THE PUBIC HAIR BLUES

3 guys
living with
1 woman
it aint easy
especially when
the 1 woman
doesn't dig
the living habits
of the 3 guys &
is not about to provide
maid service
you know how it is
hank, louie & i
figure the dishes
can wait til tomorrow
& marie wants them done
now
her latest thing
is the bathtub
you turkeys, she screams
i want the crud
& the pubic hairs
cleaned up
before I get in
that tub

like i said
it aint easy
hank's picked up his guitar
again &
is working on a new song
called
the pubic hair blues &
me & louie
are trying to figure out
how we ever managed
before she moved
in

NIGHT OF THE BLACK LUNG

It was the night of the black lung.
Shakespearian comics
sat at mustard-stained tables
while magic chessboards
wiggled thru the crowds
Carnivals came to life
in the form of paper mannequins
and five-dimensional spirits
were afraid to go out in the world
because it was raining.
Double-knits pranced by
with their hairspray revolution.
In the solitude of madness
a virgin deer trembled
while the armies of derange
sneered.
The candle burned
while outside
lunatics with pushbuttons
played almighty
never consulting
only deciding.
The world was a holocaust
but inside
crumpled cigarettes
floated methodically
and outside it was still raining.
Energy raged with nowhere to go.
The night of the black lung
was upon us.

NERVOUS BREAKDOWNS

in the paper today/
     a curious item
     about a woman

     suing a supermarket
     claiming
a squeaky shopping
     cart
     gave her
     a nervous
breakdown

     ah!   the possibilities

     the next time
     you're stuck
in rush hour
     traffic
& some clown
     starts
honking his horn

     jump out of
     your car
     & sue

the bastard

YOU JUST NEVER KNOW

as a kid
he was always
a little different

& one time
chased my brother
around the yard

with a baseball bat
if we ever tried
to retaliate

he'd fall
to the ground
call his mother

start crying
& say we pushed him
she'd come running

screaming yelling
& giving us hell
sometimes

for kicks
he'd pedal his bike
down a hill

fast as he could
& run straight
into a tree

whenever
he got really mad
he'd stand

& bang his head
repeatedly
against a wall

in high school
he once tried
to rape my sister

nothing ever came of it
probably because our families
were friends & no one
wanted to make
an issue of it
i don't know

maybe he knew something
we didn't
you just never know

my brother and i
are both unemployed
& last i heard

he was a cop

PUT UP OR SHUT UP

if you are so damn miserable
elite & independent
then prove it
perform that final act
of self determination
kill yourself
slash your wrists
take 350 downers
shoot up some drano
you know, "do your thing"
otherwise, quit your bitching
nobody is listening

REQUIEM FOR A LOST FEELING

Sitting in the rainy cluttered city square
   in the dark of evening madness
      feeling like a junkie
      in the springtime of relief

Laughing like the ignorant beast
   in the forest of jumbled joy
      feeling like an owl
      in the autumn of wisdom

Something smells
   and i feel it
     oozing down my leg
      in a mist of sleeze
Must be
   i'm losing my senses
   to a fickle bird
     of orgasmic anarchy

THE POEM I NEVER WROTE

it's not often
that I have a stroke
of genius but here
i was having it
when my girl
asked me for
a glass of water so
i went to the kitchen
& got her the water
& when i sat down
she started rubbing
my leg & i forgot
what in hell
i was thinking

CONVERSATIONS ABOUT CONVERSATIONS

we sit and talk
  in a circle
   about how we sit
     and talk in a circle

get up sit down
  think about
   what it is like to
     get up sit down

pass the word
  that the word
   is being
    passed

we joke about
  jokes that
   we joked about
    in our jokes

KIDS

i don't make
a lotta friends
with this opinion
in fact
people get
downright hostile
you'd think
i was claiming
baseball causes cancer
or george washington
use to cornhole
alexander hamilton
you see,
i don't like kids
when i look at them
i don't see all this
freespiritcreativeenergybeautifulasthewind
bullshit
i see
a future drunk
a future mass murderer
a future computer programmer
a future soldier
a future mortician

a future highway fatality
a future child molester
a future corporate exec
a future wife beater
a future junkie
a future Nixon
even a future asshole
like me & then
i get depressed
& it ruins
my whole day

ABOUT ONCE A MONTH

it builds up
so much
that i finally
explode
i jump
in her shit
she jumps
in mine
i don't perceive
what she's perceiving
she doesn't perceive
what i'm perceiving
on & on we go
2 simultaneous
one-way conversations
like she's yelling
to a 3rd person
in the room
& i'm shouting
at a 4th
finally
around nine
something good
comes on the tube

& we call a time out
around ten
i'm nuzzling up
to her saying
i'm sorry
she says she's sorry
& we agree
we don't want
to fight anymore
& before the night is out
we fuck
& somehow table
the entire problem
for at least
another
month

THE REVEREND WYSS SPEAKS

hey friends!
forget
all that jive
you've been fed
forget
reverend moon
billy graham
the zen masters
the jesus freaks
the crazy rabbis
the christian scientists
the maharishi
the hare krishnas
& all the other
drugstore gurus
i got the truth!
y' hear!
i got the truth!
You've been conned
god is a little old man
with white hair &
a crooked back
he lives in the woods
in a rundown shack
& runs around
24 hours a day
7 days a week
52 weeks a year
with a pair of scissors
in one hand &

a pile of strings
in the other
& do you know
who the strings are?
well, brothers and sisters
the strings are you and me
he puts 'em up &
he cuts 'em down
it's outa his control
& outa ours too
snip snip
& we're gone
believe me, brothers & sisters
i got the truth!
& if you don't believe me
send $4.99 & a SASE to
9415 Westheimer #317C
Houston, Texas 77063

HALLELUJAH!!!

POTATO CHIP

i am
a hopeless
daydream
lurking
somewhere in
the armpit
of my country
like
a potato chip
hiding in a box
knowing all too well
that outside
something bigger
than it
waits silently
to devour
or
crush it

ONE MAN'S VIEW
OF THE GREAT AMERICAN DREAM

something about
driving to a parking lot
at midnight
to make a living
that makes you
think
about your life
& what it's become
you know,
like your life
was suppose
to be more
than this
maybe even mean something
but then
you wake up
one morning
with a diploma
stuffed
in your back pocket
searching for a lost dream
like some drunk
trying to remember
where
he left his wallet

MOVE LIKE A BUTTERFLY, STING LIKE A BEE

things have been going
pretty bad lately
in fact
downright rotten
& probably enuf to
make most people
buckle under
but not me
i'm stealing a technique
from muhammed ali
the rope-a-dope
for the 1st 7 rounds
i'm letting life slug away
i'm taking its best punches
& then
come the 8th round
i'm gonna knock it
flat
on its ass

STAND UP AND BE COUNTED

there are times
i wish
i could fly
you know, soar
above the bullshit
look down & laugh
maybe even carry
a sackful of elephant turds
& when I'm high enough
above the madness
let it drop
yeh, i know
it's not much
in the way
of social protest
but hell
what can one person do?

FOR ROBERT FRIEDMAN, AGE 43
OR:
YOU CAN'T BEAT THE SYSTEM
(A FOUND POEM)

when chicago police busted him
for panhandling in front of a bus station
he was carrying a briefcase that contained
$24,087 in small bills
later a judge committed him to
a mental institution to protect him
from thugs who might be after his cash
since then he has had his savings
eaten away by hospital fees & doctor's bills
for treatment ordered by the court &
by $800/mo. rent the state charges him
at the mental facility & he even had to pay
the fees for the lawyer who argued
he be committed

says his lawyer:

> "he worked since he was 11 & was
> a very good clerk-typist who at
> one time took shorthand at 100
> words/minute. he lived frugally
> his entire life & saved every
> penny he could. he wore old clothes
> lived in an $80/mo. hotel room ate
> day-old bread & fruit. his only
> obsession was saving money & if he
> didn't have that money he's be a
> free man today."

A LESSON IN PEDESTIAN SAFETY

Ralph Bloomfield was lying half-asleep in front of his T.V. set with a half-empty can of Budweiser resting snug on his protruding stomach. The door of his first floor apartment was open and Ralph could hear the steady buzz of the mid-afternoon traffic as it ran to and fro on Elm Street.

Suddenly, like a bolt of lightning, a dark green Oldsmobile crashed through the wall of his living room, leaving tire tracks on the carpet and completely mowing over Ralph.

Whew, what was that, thought Ralph, as the automobile disappeared into the landscape made visible by its hasty exit through the back wall.

Ralph dusted off his T-shirt and dungarees, and struggled slowly to his feet. A young man in a blue uniform appeared where the front wall had once stood. He shook a disapproving finger at Ralph.

"My good man," he said, "You simply must be more careful and keep an eye out for automobiles."

I KNOW IT'S JUST A THEORY, BUT ...

we are being bought & sold
                caught up
      in some grand conspiracy
monty hall is our messiah
tim leary is handing out our names
      like hits of acid &
                the president
is thinking of sending ground troops
      into scotland
                a few of us
are trying to sift thru
      the madness
                while the rest
are marching straight ahead
      like
            hitler's youth &
i wish my ant-perspirant
      would
            keep
                me
                      dry ...

HOW TO BECOME
A USEFUL MEMBER OF SOCIETY

the best way to start
is to close all your doors
shut your windows &
draw your blinds
then check for any light
that may be coming in
perhaps you'll notice some
creeping thru the bottom of a door
if so, grab a towel &
snuff it out
then turn off all the lights
next, to be on the safe side
take a handkerchief or maybe
an old t-shirt & blindfold
yourself
then close your eyes
as tight as you can
find a comfortable spot
on the sofa & relax
you've just joined the human race

I GUESS YOU COULD SAY I'M DESPERATE

look, she says
i know it's not a great job
but don't you think
you should take it
afterall
you've been outa work
for nearly 4 months now
& the rent is due
& the bills are starting
to pile up
you can't afford
to be choosy
she's probably right
but i still don't like it
but i still give in
monday
i report to work
i fill out a W-4
& they show me the timeclock
i punch in & they lead me
to where I'll be working
okay fella, says the foreman
let's get started
he tells me
to drop my pants
to the floor
bend over
grab my ankles
& grit my teeth
then, one by one

everyone in the company
who holds a higher position
than me (& that's everyone)
proceeds to take his turn
it's not exactly
my idea of a great job
but they do pay
$2.30 an hour

EVER NOTICE?

ever notice
how some people
have that look
a distant
troubled look
that tells you
something is wrong
but they're not quite sure
what
they've got a box seat
by the 3rd base dugout
for the 7th game
of the world series
it's the 9th inning
game's tied
2 outs
bases loaded
3-2 count
the pitcher
is in his windup
& they're not even
paying attention

OUTSIDE

outside …

among the lingering trees
staring at the power lines
fearing the nine-to-fivers
loathing shopping malls
rooting for the underdog
the impoverished, the pervert
& the proverbial fucked-over
every day is sunday

… for i must rest

THE GAP

marie touches me with
tender particles of her understanding
go if you must, she says
take a month's vacation
leave behind your job
this apartment & me
just come back, i'll be here
she casts herself in the role
of florence nightingale
never realizing that
i resent her
resent her inability
to suffer along with me
i want to scream
doesn't this life
suffocate you TOO?
christ, i don't want
to split & suffer alone
spending a few midnights
in the darkness of an interstate
my thumb out & rain falling
maybe getting laid once or twice
while she stays home

& has the time of her life
swimming in flowers
fancy restaurants
& 24-carat dicks
only to return home to
an everwidening gap
christ, i want to close
that miserable gap
want her to suffer with me
want her to understand
that suffering cannot be parceled
into neat little one month vacations

THE GAME

is called gunfighter
costs a quarter
& is by far
the most popular
in the bar
it takes 2
to play &
you each get a cowboy
with a gun
& 2 levers
to work with
1 for aiming
& shooting
your gun
the other
for moving
your cowboy
behind a cactus
around a covered wagon
up & down
dodging bullets
emptying your gun
avoid ricochets
taking shots
in your head
in your stomach
in your foot

you fire away
for 60 seconds
& see how many times
you can hit
the other dude
& when you finish
you notice
your forehead
is perspiring
your palms
are clammy
your heart is
beating too fast
& you're giggling
like some sickie
in a museum
of horrors

AN EVENING
IN THE GARDEN OF DYING FLOWERS

In the garden of dying flowers,
the sun rarely shines.
Flowers are falling slowly to the ground;
stale, stagnant – without nourishment.
Flowers have stopped growing.
In time they will become dust;
blowing in the wind,
   making room for more dying flowers.

The outpost of desolation faces. Have been sitting here for hours. Jukebox pounding. TV a chimerical haze of reds, blues and greens as its image struggles desperately toward me through the grey cancer smoke rising from the bar like morning mist over a spring lake. Spring. I know it's Spring. Calendar dictates April. Yet, here at the outpost, there are no seasons. I've been nursing this beer too long – revoltingly piss warm.

Just passing through. Between yesterday and tomorrow. Just a stopover – a visit to some old friends in this town of malt and hops. When I left fifteen months ago, the same blank faces were sitting on the same blank bar stools.

"Hey Gary, how 'bout another beer", I shout as the short, broad-shouldered bartender moves within ear range.

Who cares, I'll be hitching out tomorrow. Watching slow death work methodically, unde-tected, behind the scenes, between the lines, under the stools, behind the pool tables, in the men's room. The last time I pissed, I absorbed the crude graffiti. Don't throw cigarette butts in the toilet, it makes them soggy and hard to smoke.

Firm, friendly hand resting on my shoulder. The grinning teeth of Pete staring me smack dab in the middle of my consciousness. I swim over to his face returning the smile.

"Hey you sonofabitch, you look like you could use another beer. GARY! HEY! GARY! Give this bastard another beer."

"Thanks Pete. Pull up a seat."

Pete grabbing a stool a few feet away. Maneuvering his six feet four inch frame onto it. Pete has the thin but solid body of an athlete. His string-like brown hair reaches down to and licks his shoulders. His reddish-brown beard steps to the background, making room for his blood-shot eyes. He tosses thirty cents across the top of the bar. I now have an army of two beers challenging me. Pete shifts on his stool, as if putting the money down has upset his equilibrium.

"So you're leaving tomorrow, eh Kirk?"

I nod, producing a tired cliché. "Yeh, time to hit the road again."

Sitting a few minutes in our silence. Pete a picture of hypnotized concentration as he zeros in on the TV, He has lost his smile and fingers his near-empty glass like a nervous child. My head totally immersed in the music screaming from the jukebox. Can't help noticing how too much noise produces silence. The Silence of Stentor. Everyone here living in the 20's, captives of a silent picture, drinking and absorbed into silence. Jukebox drowning out the tube. No one knows what song is playing. Mannequins tapping their feet to silence.

I watch Penelope. Another picture of concentration, lining up a shot on the pool table. Concentration. Style. Gentle stroke of right arm. Orange five-ball in corner pocket. She stands there for a moment, staring intently at her shot. Half-smile on her narrow face gives away her feeling of satisfaction.

"You know Kirk," resumes Pete, "I'd like to get out of this place."

I glide back into Pete's world. "Why don't you, then?"

Pete gulps down the remaining beer.

The question has been put. He knows the answer. So do I. For the sake of social grace and, most likely, something to pass the time, the conversation continues. I buy Pete another beer. We drink.

Pete begins, shaking his head. He spits forthI-don't-know, Penelope-and-I-are-always-fighting, everything-is-bringing-me-down, can't-get-a-fucking- job, nothing-to-do-but-come-down-here-and-drink, I-get-drunk-every-night.........

A sad, resigned look reflects from his eyes. I know he wouldn't be telling me his problems if he wasn't so drunk. The TV blares with a symphony of voices. A song has just ended on the jukebox and an eerie silence permeates the room while everyone is waiting for the next song to drown out their private conversations. Penelope comes over and taps dejected Pete on the shoulder. She has finished her pool game. Her voice is soft, but carries with it a touch of coldness.

"Do you want to start home now, Pete?"

Pete snaps from deep within his world.

"I don't know if I'm going home tonight."

Penelope is standing there with a blank look on her face. She glances toward me, shrugs her shoulders and walks to the corner of the bar to order another drink. I find myself wanting to fuck her.

Pete and I resume our conversation. His voice tells me how he wishes he could just pick up and leave, come and go as he pleases. I am getting drunk. Another song blasts forth and I raise my voice to be heard. I pronounce another tired cliché. It tells Pete that there is nothing stopping him, if he wants to go somewhere, just go, it's as simple as that. We are all great philosophers when we have a few drinks under our belts.

The conversation becomes an endless barrage of excuses, fears, rationalizations. Pete pauses.

"You know what I mean, don't you Kirk?"

My head nods in the affirmative. Pete finishes off his beer, stands up and moves toward the men's room. There are two people ahead of him, so he makes himself comfortable by leaning with his left elbow on a defenseless pinball machine.

Penelope slides out of nowhere, replacing Pete on the empty stool. Pale blue eyes smiling into mine.

"How's your pool game goin' tonight?" I volunteer.

A flowing, slow smile. "Oh, not too bad."

Preliminaries finish. A mass of seriousness begins a slow materialization through her facial pores. I feel my neutrality being threatened. She speaks with her eyes frozen on the glossy bar.

"What was Pete complaining about to you?"

I like Penelope, complete with her frail, little-girl aura. My mind performs another cliché, unspoken: Penelope wouldn't hurt a fly. Jukebox continues its steady pound. I defend my neutrality.

"Oh, nothing much."

Penelope deciphers my lie and resolves to silence. She seems content to leave her eyes on top of the bar. She wants to talk, will talk, does talk. Her eyes remain on the bar. Her voice forces its way through the thunderous silence to reach me.

"I've been talking to Marion and she says I can move in with her. I think I'm going to sleep at her place tonight. Pete and I just don't get along."

Her eyes still refuse to meet mine. She arches her head back and pours another shot of novocain down her throat. There is little conviction in her gentle vocality. Pete and

Penelope are always splitting up. I hold steadfast to my neutral ground. Penelope perceives this and attempts to change the course of the conversation. Her eyes finally acknowledge mine.

"Pete told me that he was thinking of taking off with you."

Here at the outpost, everyone is always thinking of leaving. I slink back into the confab. I speak a truth.

"That's news to me."

So much for Pete's idle threats to Penelope. She switches to the lighter side.

"When are you leaving?"

"Tomorrow, I guess."

I order two more beers. Penelope takes out a cigarette. I react with my Pavlov dog routine, reaching in my breast pocket for a fag, too. I light hers, then mine. A grey haze invests us and Penelope continues.

"Kirk, I'm going nuts. Living with Pete has become unbearable. I feel like I'm a prisoner. He's so fucking possessive. Whenever he sees me talking with another guy, he goes crazy. I'm tired of all his bullshit."

Only now do I notice Pete reentering and lurking in our world. Having come out of the men's room and seen us together, he does a molasses stroll by us, culminating in a fuming lean at the far end of the bar. He orders another beer. Penelope mumbles.

"See what I mean? He's even pissed off

because I'm talking to you."

I step forth as the devil's advocate. (feeble attempt)

"Oh, I don't think that has anything to do with it."

Our beers are gone. I order two more. Penelope counters.

"Oh yes it does. He's like this all the time. And besides, he's constantly drinking. Whenever we get around to talking things over, he's usually too drunk to make any sense or talk things out reasonably."

Getting drunk and tired. Okay Penelope. Okay Pete. Enough's enough. The jukebox. The smoke. The light at the end of the tunnel. Gulping my beer. Keeping my balance. Let me retreat to neutral ground. Still, dear friend Penelope, I'd like to fuck you. You know it too, don't you Pete?

Pete groping a curly-headed blonde at the end of the bar. Penelope's hand suddenly in mine. She sums it up.

"I'm not going home with Pete tonight."

I'd love to … but … I'd love to … but … I'd love to … but … but …

"Penelope, I have to piss. Be right back."

I down my beer and begin my temporary escape. Walking on a merry-go-round. Legs unsteady, unreliable. Edging my way through the drunken masses … keep it together. My first miscalculation befalls. Back side of pool cue jabs my stomach. I'm sorry, excuse me, didn't mean to fuck up your shot. Amorphous faces crystallizing on all sides. Voices diffusing from within fuzzy lineaments. HOW YA DOIN' KIRK. HEY YOU MOTHER YOU LOOK A LITTLE FUCKED UP. Excuse me. MAN YOU SHOULD HAVE SEEN THIS CHICK, SHE ... Excuse me, excuse me, I just wanna piss. HEY ____ YOU WANNA COME OVER TO MY PLACE 'N PARTY. Almost there now. Hope there isn't a line ...

"Hi Kirk, I didn't know you were in town."

I try to focus on the friendly smile before me. Room doing a slow spin. It looks like ... by god it is ... it's Lisa.

"Hi Lisa, howya doin'?"

She gives me a hug and hearty kiss on my cheek. Damn she looks nice tonight! My hands stroke the curvature of her back.

"Listen Lisa, I'm going to piss my pants if I stand here much longer. I'll be right back."

Sure Kirk, she sneers, pinching my ass. The plot thickens as I float to the head. I open the door of peeled blue paint and my eyes meet a fusillade of words scrawled crassly across the puke green plasterboard walls. ALL FRATS SUCK. FOR A GOOD BLOW JOB CALL MARY 472-6241. THE ONLY DOPE WORTH SHOOTING IS NIXON. JACK ROBERTS IS A QUEER ... I watch the yellow arch of relief as it does a swan dive into the porcelain bowl. Molecules of water and urine unite and leap up at the walls of the toilet. Ah ... hh ... hhh.

Pillows of smoke ... faces without features ...

music ... noise ... engulfing me as I leave the relief closet. Let's see, I was talking to Lisa, wasn't I? Probing the crowd, unable to make out her outline. Pete performing all the proper barroom courtships, still groping hopefully for the curly-headed blonde. Lisa lost somewhere in the one-dimensional outline of drunks, bartenders, pool players, TV watchers, philosophers, loners and losers. Fighting my way through the confusion ... pawing and poking anyone and everything in my path. HOW YA DOIN' KIRK. HEY YOU MOTHER YOU LOOK A LITTLE FUCKED UP. Excuse me. MAN YOU SHOULD HAVE SEEN THIS CHICK, SHE ... Excuse me, excuse me, I just wanna sit down. HEY ____ YOU WANNA COME OVER TO MY PLACE LATER 'N PARTY. The waiting face of Penelope. Now I remember. Isn't this what I'm trying to escape? There must be a way out.

Penelope touches me with "I'd almost given up on you." I return the touch with "I got lost." Penelope laughs. I smile. Now what? replaced by Whew! with the deliverance of Lisa from barspace unknown. My existence nearly ceases as the two friends commence dialogue. Seriousness emerges, blending Penelope's tired story with the arrival of Lisa's interest. I want to be serious/interested/concerned (too) but it seems so silly. Lisa drunker than Penelope and I combined, but maintaining herself better than either of us. My mind performs a thought: Lisa is still the same alcoholic she was fifteen months ago. Music so loud. Pool balls crack through the music. The voice of Penelope/Lisa lost in barroom pandemonium. Music … crack of pool balls … music … crack of pool balls … between songs, the roar of TV voices. My mind meandering, my eyes keenly aware. I watch the thin creamy bony fingers of Lisa as they perform a gesture. A laugh from Penelope. A common truth from Lisa produces an affirmative nod from Penelope. Pete passes through the movie for a fraction of a flash, performing a glare which Penelope chooses not to notice. I perform intents: the intent of leaving tomorrow … the intent of not getting involved any further in the Pete/Penelope Problem … the intent of fucking Lisa. A pause in the conversation unfolds, producing a vacant space between words which someone or something must fill. I make my play.

"Lisa, you're looking good. Whatcha been up to?"

Her attention turns to me.

"Oh nothing much," she says.

Another vacant space between words which this time no one chooses to fill. Finally, Penelope.

"My quarter's up."

Penelope lifting her petite frame and gliding toward the pool table. My eyes execute as if a telescopic lens, zeroing in on Lisa, making everything but her an intangible blur. My brain shrieking: go forth Nimrod! Realizing I must make a move before total inebriation sets in. Lisa's eyes meet mine and we perform ocular intercourse.

"Lisa," I slur, "I've always wanted to fuck you."

So be it. The intent has surfaced and spilled forth from my tongue, flowing in a thousand directions, beyond recall.

Lisa's face becoming warm, flushing red, gathering up the flying particles of an honest declaration. A blushing piquancy emerges. Our eyes touch.

"Why haven't you told me this before?"

Suddenly from the midst of oblivion, the form of Penelope checks in, confessing her eavesdrop.

"What are you waiting for?"

Uneasy laughter bellowing throughout the outpost, passing unheard by the caricatures of drunks, bartenders, pool players, TV watchers, philosophers, loners and losers.

"Yeh, what are we waiting for?" I shout while Lisa and Penelope exchange female smiles. Lisa presto into seriousness.

"Kirk, when are you leaving?"

"Tomorrow morning. Why?"

Lisa glancing at her watch.

"Why that hardly gives us enough time to undress."

Pause followed by another pause.

"Why don't you stay another day or two?"

Smile spreading across my face like melting butter. Already imagining Lisa's long legs wrapped like macaroni around my flesh. "Let's get our coats."

Lisa and I moving hand-in-hand like two desperadoes toward the coat racks, shoving the dead wood of bodies from our path. Laughing like fourteen year old kids on a first date, two stray cats in heat. Grabbing through the pool table ... moving ... fighting ... the door, yes the door.

"Kirk?"

"Yeh?"

"You are going to stay another day or two, aren't you?"

I smile and nod. Of course I am Lisa. What's another day or two? The garden ... well, I can always leave the garden ... anytime I want ... yeh, I'll leave the garden the day after tomorrow ... what's the hurry ... maybe next week ...

As we jetstream toward the door, I catch a glimpse of Pete and Penelope sitting at a table screaming at one another, each trying desperately to be heard. Ah yes ... the garden of dying flowers. I'll be leaving soon.

OTHER SMALL PRESS
APPEARANCES
IN THE 1970'S

a day is a lifetime on an interstate highway

zooming & zipping
along cement
slithering as a snake
thru green pastures
of america countryside
in a capsule
traveling
seventy mph
listening to
a singing dashboard
& wanting
to get there

BROKEN DOWN CHEVY

something about these crazy people
the ones who have never
adjusted who have never
been able to suppress
their anger I watch
this old man sputter
past the 7-11 like
a broken down chevy
make obscene gestures
at the passing cars
& yell JESUS CHRIST!
like he just hit his
thumb with a hammer
his long white hair
is in a frenzy & he
is waving a brown
paper bag when he
spots me on the side
walk and gives me the
finger & shouts STUPID
MOTHERFUCKER!
for just a second
I want to walk
over to him put
a hand on his
shoulder tell him

I understand I am
on his side
but that thought passes
& I find myself
walking faster
away from him
away from what he represents
away from someone who looks
a little too much
like me

DAILY I GO TO JOB INTERVIEWS

only today it is worse
I'm trying to convince this creep
that I am a believer
that I want this job
which I really don't want
& make him believe
that I am the man
he is looking for
when practically any clown off the street
Is better suited for it than me

Actually, it has been going pretty well
He has scored with a few
left hooks
but I've countered with a couple
of solid rights
I'm getting good at this
It has almost become a hobby

But all of a sudden
he is asking me a question
& I feel as if the lights
are going out
There is a strange persistent ringing
in my left ear

Am I going mad?
Is this one of those acid flashbacks
that I've been expecting
for years?
His words seem to be at the end
Of a long tunnel
I am crazy
I know it

Daily I go to job interviews
It has become a job
in itself

WALKING THE TIGHTROPE

Who is REALLY crazy?
Oh sure, some people
THINK they know the answer
THINK they can find it
at the school library
or in a computer printout
the priests
the shrinks
the cops
even your favorite bartender
figure they've got
some special insight
but still
the debate goes on
& I find myself
reading the morning paper
fascinated by a black gunman
who grabs a hostage
& demands
that all white people
leave the face of the earth
& everyone is labeling him crazy
a terrorist, a nut
yet here I am
digging what he's saying
except thinking that

I'd include
blacks browns reds yellows greens purples
& possibly
all mosquitos

each day
a lot of us
walk that tightrope
balancing ourselves
on the edge
of sanity
& it only takes
one push
or a gust of wind
like with me
I'm on my 31st job
& if they were to fire me
or my 2nd wife
were to run off
with an insurance salesman
or some turd
were to steal my quarter
off the pool table
one too many times
I might just lose it
& then they'd be calling ME
crazy

MY ARMY

Last night I found myself running as fast as my legs would carry me. Running with fear.

Behind me legions of half-man/half-beast creatures were in hot pursuit, screaming violently with spears raised above their pointed heads.

As I scurried up and down hills, over plains, through pastures and across oceans, I saw the sky dotted with hundreds of gigantic prehistoric birds. I knew that both the birds and the half-man/half-beasts viewed me as another of their helpless prey.

As I reached the peak of a tremendous mountain, I turned and sneered. Then, at the top of my lungs, I shouted "CHARGE!" Suddenly, as if descending from Heaven, thousands of phantom jets appeared on the horizon. Millions of tanks swept across the plains. The sea swarmed with battle ships. Armies moved in from the north, south, east and west.

I sat down on the mountain and watched the show. It was over in a matter of minutes. Soon, every prehistoric bird and every half-man/half-beast creature was a footnote in history. As the dust cleared, I stood up and brushed myself off. Then I went home.

Later, I told my friend Heinrich what had happened. He was quite philosophical.

"You know," he said, "it would be great if everyone could have an army like yours. It sure would make things easier."

METAMORPHOSIS II

As Gregor Samsa awoke one morning
from uneasy dreams, he found
himself transformed in his bed
into a giant hamburger.

He was lying on one half
of a toasted sesame seed bun
& when he lifted his head
he could see that his stomach
was covered with shredded lettuce
two pickle slices, a dab of catsup
& the other half of the toasted
sesame seed bun.

Gregor Samsa yawned
& then went back to sleep.

PARANOIA

i'm surrounded by little green men
i can't see them
but i know they're here
i can smell them
i can hear them

come on honey, my wife says
it's late
come to bed

i can't, i say
i'm surrounded

o don't be silly, she says
it's only your imagination
now come to bed

where's my gun, i shout
you don't have one, she says
you don't even know how to use one

jesus christ, i scream
what am i going to do?

you're going to come to bed, she says

ok, i answer
i'll be right there

when i walk in
i find a little green man
in bed with my wife

it's no use
i can't fight it

i jump in
& make it a threesome

PERFECTION

getting tired of being force-fed
perfection everytime
i turn on the tv
watch a movie
pick up a magazine
getting tired of
perfect cops
perfect robbers
perfect men
perfect women
perfect heros
perfect villans
perfect families
perfect businessmen
perfect secretaries
perfect commies
perfect bigots
perfect blacks
perfect hippies
perfect smiles
perfect tears
perfect tits
perfect cocks
perfect cunts
perfect desires
perfect ...
     perfect ...
        perfect ...
i'm beginning to feel inadequate

ICE CREAM SANDWICH

The room is glowing phosphorescent red
for you are in the ice cream sandwich
of hippydom with day-glo streamers
nothing to lose but a day's sleep
so smoke smoke smoke
groove on electronic sounds
talk about Frank Zappa
and how this hash
really gets you wasted, man

Dropped out but drifting
in the ozone sphere of nothing
neither here nor there
slowly fizzling
waiting for the next concert
and some trips in the mail
trying to be in the realm
of freedom forming happenings
and spacing out, of course

Hey man, know what day it is?

POEM TO MY FIRST WIFE

i never told you
about the time
you drove 20 miles
to see your mother
& how i sat home
playing with the cat
entertaining strange visions
of you skidding &
sliding off the road
crashing into a ditch
i ran it over & over
in my mind
till it became real

later,
when I heard the car
pull in the driveway
i was disappointed
knowing then
there would be
no easy way
out

THOUGHT FOR THE DAY

wonder
how many people
there are across america
waiting at home for
michael anthony convinced
they've been forgotten
by the american dream
yet still hoping
it will return
to rescue
them

DIALOGUE TIL THE END

Some of us will still be talking
when the silent autumn arrives
We will still devise
words,
formulas,
experiments,
and excuses
for man's dilemma
The fire will rage
and our minds
will still be burning with questions
of why it all happened
Burn, baby, burn!

SO MUCH FOR FLOWER POWER

where's my dope
    where's my money
where's my hope
    where's my honey

THESE HARRY TRUMAN JUNKIES

are getting to be dangerous
the way they run around
screaming
harry truman
mainlining
harry truman songs
harry truman books
harry truman plays
harry truman movies

even the president carries
a picture of good old harry
in his wallet
hell, you'd think
it was the second coming

maybe i'm weird but
i keep thinking that
it was old harry who
ordered the bombing
of hiroshima
back in those days before
walter cronkite, panavision
& living color

for the life of me
i can't remember
how many died
60,000? 100,000?
a million?
but that has to count
for something
doesn't it?

WRITERS

little distended egos
      sitting in seedy shanties
      busily shifting words
   in a mad frenzy
   of

gotta get that message across
      fancying distant shores
      where the forests
      stand on their toes
   and

listen to the inside stories
      which are neon signs
      in the city square
      by the statues
      that

have been erected

BETTER LIVING THRU CHEMISTRY

every bone in my body aches
my eyes burn like hot coals
my legs hang like branches
on a dead tree
but the amphetamine
beating of my heart
proves once again
the wonder of being
a drug child of
the twentieth century

THE INTELLIGENT ELECTORATE

my grandmother, a lifelong republican
wouldn't vote for tom dewey
cuz he wore a moustache
my dad just told me he doesn't like
the way jerry brown dresses
i've heard jfk carried the sex appeal crowd
i imagine abe lincoln lost votes
cuz he was skinny &
william howard taft cuz he was fat
it's been like that for 200 years
george washington probably lost a few
cuz he wore a wig (the anti-sissy vote)
now it appears jimmy carter has the support
of the american dental association
at least my conscience is clear
i don't carry those kind of prejudices
no, not ME
i wouldn't vote
for ONE of those sonsofbitches

HOME & ALONE

you want to be with me
but not badly enough
to come home
i want to be with you
but not badly enough
to go find you
is there something
i don't see
i don't feel
& what about tomorrow nite
will i be out
& you waiting
will you talk to the radio
like i am doing now
you know, the radio
keeps talking to me
as if i wasn't here

A DREAM I ONCE HAD ABOUT THE GREAT CATSUP SHORTAGE

billy breedlove sitting dormant in front of tv
beercan resting lazy on the white t-shirt of his
stomach
six o'clock news – walter cronkite jarbling
lives, deaths, dollars, depression
tidbits of media sounds penetrate
billy breedlove's benign walls
price of catsup skyrocketing
catsup shortage, presidential speech
after a word from our sponsor
(THOUGHT)
        someday a war
        will be brought to us
        by a toothpaste
        with sex appeal

in the kitchen jennifer breedlove making dinner
ground beef deluxe, billy's favorite
french fries ….

great stone face of president materializes on tv
screen
somber, my fellow americans
is with a heavy heart i speak to you tonite
jarble jarble economy falling apart
jabble jabble this is a time in our history
when we must make sacrifices as a people
jarble jabble we in the great stone castles of ac/dc
have been working our hearts out

jabble jabble to keep the price of catsup down
efforts have failed
jarble jarble

echo of jennifer breedlove from kitchen
dinner's ready, come & get it
picture of stability
as she glides
across kitchen floor
burgers in hand ....

back on the tube
great white father announces creation
of commission to study great catsup shortage
cries from the kitchen
dinner's ready dinner's ready
president introduces tall handsome savior
(robot smile intact)
richard angelo stable
manager mcdonald's hamburgers
binghamton new york
vast experience
in jabble jarble science of hamburgers
qualifies & gives me great confidence
in his jarble jabble ability
to act decisively
in this great catsup shortage
place your fate in the hands of a hamburger king

billy's blood rising
sound currents from kitchen
dinner's ready
& now mr. stable ….

billy's shoe flying thru the tube
pop fizzle shatter smash
anger stalks toward the kitchen
shouting what's for dinner what's for dinner
jennifer sings burgers fries
billy looking at steaming burgers fries plate
incomplete
goes to refrigerator
great white slab swings open
catsup where's the catsup
no catsup where's the catsup
we're out of catsup billy
what!!!! it can't be it can't be
billy sinking into kitchen chair
face buried in hands
energy moving into action ….

(ACTION)

billy grabbing hat & coat & planting hasty kiss
on roseate cheek of jennifer

wind whipping & snow soaring
billy marching onward

billy a thrust of energy
bursting thru walls of the great supermarket
james cagney finger in coat pocket
proclaiming this is a stickup

humble supermarket manager
telling blue-face clerks
give him everything he wants

billy proudly:
i'll take the largest damn truck you have
& all the catsup in the fucking store

mealy-mouth clerks salute yes sir
& scamper for the shelves
confusion ensues
catsup delivered

put it in the truck shouts billy

you heard the gentleman
orders the supermarket manager

make it snappy screams billy

truck loaded in keystone cop fashion
billy driving into the dawn in a flash

(SIX O'CLOCK NEWS REVISITED)

billy breedlove sitting dormant in front of tv
beercan resting lazy on the white t-shirt of his
stomach
six o'clock news – walter cronkite jarbling
lives, deaths, dollars, depression .....

NEWS FROM HOMEFRONT ..... YESTERDAY A
MAN
HELD UP THE GREAT SUPERMARKET AT
GUNPOINT
IN AMERICA STEALING A TRUCK & STORE'S
COMPLETE
SUPPLY OF CATSUP ..... HOURS LATER
JUBLILANT CITIZENS
REPORTED A MAN WITH A CRAZED LOOK
FITTING
DESCRIPTION OF CATSUP THIEF HANDING OUT
FREE BOTTLES OF CATSUP ON THE STREETS
OF AMERICA .....

billy breedlove smiling
what's for dinner
jennifer sings burgers fries
billy dusting off his american flag
& heading for a meal
        befitting a hero
                in contemporary america

THE CRITIC

Fred hates my stuff
says it's the worst
shit he's ever read
yesterday, as usual
he stopped by
to raid my refrigerator
& I told him
I had just received
$2.50 for 3 poems
I think you're overpaid he said
as he grabbed a beer &
a couple of sandwiches

THE PRETTIEST SMILE

my grandmother
entered my picture
in a kid with
the prettiest smile
contest when
i was 3

the way it worked
was they put all
the pictures in
the window of
the local hardware
store with a jar
beneath each one &
the kid with
the most money
in his or her jar
won

my grandmother
filled the jar
with all the change
she had accumulated
in her lifetime &

i'll be damned
if i didn't win
i don't know who
got all the money
but i do know
it was the last
contest i ever
won

EDDIE LOWMAN
(found poem)

56 yrs old
living for 2 yrs
in the stairwells & corridors
of sheriff's dept hdqters
busted on thanksgiving
& sent to jail
for 90 days
so he won't be alone
on christmas
apparently subsisted
on sandwiches
provided by janitors
& by rummaging
thru garbage cans
deputies said
the gray-haired
sad-eyed man
told them
he has given up
on life
had a dollar bill
& some napkins
in his pocket
but no shoes
the 1st nite in jail
chose to sleep
on the floor
instead of on a mattress

POor man's yachT

bill is a casualty of the sixties
like the rest of us
a little burnt out
a victim of drugs
'nam & nixon
& consequently smokes
a lotta pot
& sue his old lady
she's always jumping
in his shit
but bill
he just shines her on
winking at me
& explaining
she's 7 years younger
& too young to understand
listen babe he tells her
if i was one
of those rich bastards
i'd have private jets
weekends in paris
& yachts to keep me
occupied but as it is
about all i can afford
Is a $15 bag
this aint pot babe
it's the poor man's
yacht

Greg Wyss

A PERFECT ADVERTISEMENT FOR PARALYSIS

i am
a perfect
advertisement
for paralysis
sitting here
hour after hour
doing absolutely nothing
i can
see it now
someone bursts
thru my door
announcing that
world war three
has just begun
& i suddenly
become motivated
reaching slowly
forward
to turn on
my tv

JETS VS. PATRIOTS
(found poem)

2 fans die of heart attacks

30 taken to hospital
with cuts & bruises

49 arrested

cop's jaw broken

spectator stabbed

drunken fan pisses
on back of cop giving
mouth-to-mouth resuscitation
to heart attack victim

no final score given

GOING TO WORK

6:15 AM
alarm clock echoes
leap from sleep
into world
of in-between
first undershorts
next flannel shirt
dungarees socks &
steel-toed work boots
float to bathroom
piss
wash face
brush teeth
comb hair
into kitchen
bowl of shredded wheat
w/crown of a banana &
orange blossom honey
eat eat
fast as i can
run downstairs
hope car starts
pull outa driveway

into morning flow
of work-a-day people
on cloudstream of
get-to-work-on-time
mania
park in muddy lot
hustle from car to
dark grey machine
on wall
grab timecard
insert
presto
3 minutes early!
     outside there always seems to be
     a steady drizzle of grey rain

THE GURU AND HIS CHICK

were seated next to me eating from two large platters which were steaming at the edges with roasted ants. He was a rugged, athletic-looking man in his late twenties with extremely angular features. His boyish face was marred only by a scar than ran about an inch from below his left eye to his cheekbone. He wore faded blue jeans and a white, long-sleeved muslin shirt. His chick was a fragile, emaciated woman also in her late twenties. Her curly blonde hair bounded from her head like a giant brillo pad and her pale blue eyes swelled from her face like fisheyes in an aquarium. She wore purple hot pants and an orange tank shirt which hung two sizes too big from her bony shoulders and revealed her munchkin tits.

The guru took a handful of ants and shoved them into his mouth. His chick did the same. After swallowing the ants, the guru wiped his mouth with the sleeve of his shirt.

"You see, my friend," said the guru gently, "we're into myrmecology."

"What is myrmecology?" I asked.

The guru smiled and turned to his chick who had her right hand in his lap.

"Thought you'd never ask, dude," she said. Her voice was a sensuous whisper.

"Myrmecology is a branch of entomology dealing with ants. It is our religion. We worship ants. We believe that only by studying ants can mankind learn anything about itself. We watch them, we follow them, we mimic them and we eat them." Her eyes were gleaming. "We become one with them."

"That's very interesting," I said, "but where do you go from there?"

The guru and his chick looked at one another and smiled. His chick put her hand down the guru's pants. Then they jumped up from their seats and, in a fit of frenzy, tore off each other's clothes. I was about to excuse myself when they got down on all fours and began crawling toward the nearest exit.

I was bewildered but I couldn't help but think that what they had to offer was far more interesting than Christianity. By a long shot.

THE BIG MOUTH

he enters the party
like it's hiroshima &
he's the a-bomb

his mouth

continually running
10 seconds ahead
of his brain

finally a few people
get pissed off &
tell him to shut up

but he just laughs
thinking they're only

kidding

A TOUCH OF CLASS

listen babe
if you have to
break my heart
at least do it
with a little class

    hire a savage lion
    to tear it
    from my chest
    then rent a ryder truck
    & have the lion
    drive over it
    back & forth
    til it's as flat
    as 14th century earth
    next ask the pittsburgh steelers
    to come down & stomp on it
    til you're sure
    it's dead
    then with a gleam in your eye
    & a knife in your hand
    cut it up
    into little pieces
    & invite your friends over

for hors d'oeuvres

JUST THINKING ABOUT

freaks disguised
as straights
straights as freaks
dressing up/dressing down
getting so you can't
tell the players
without a scorecard
tho i hardly give
a flying fuck
anymore
what with a cup of coffee
nearly 50 cents
what worries me
is the thought
of figuring out
how to keep
the refrigerator full
& the landlord
off my case for
another 30-40 yrs
& what if
the only answer
i can come up with

is to knock off
a bank?
what then?
i've watched enuf tv
to know the bad guys
always get caught
or even killed
which come to think of it
may not be such
a bad idea
afterall

WHO SAYS I DON'T HAVE A SENSE OF HUMOR?

the last time I saw her
she went into
her usual song & dance
it's your attitude she said
the way you always
put everything down
don't you have
a sense of humor?
why can't you smile
& look on the brighter
side instead of always
assuming the worst?
life is great
go out & enjoy the sunshine
go meet all the great
people out there
just waiting
for you
stop moaning & groaning
get rid of the beer
& throw away that goddamn
bottle of jack daniels
discover how wonderful
life can be

aaw for chrissakes i said
why don't you
get off my case?
the world is an armpit
any fool with an iq of 3
can see that
who needs it?
i'd rather live in a cave
& drink whiskey
all day
okay she said
have it your way
you're not going to
ruin my day
i'm going out in the streets
& then to the park
it's a beautiful day
the sky is blue
& i intend to enjoy it
she grabbed her frisbee
kissed me goodby
danced out the door
singing good day sunshine
& was promptly run over
by an ice cream truck

IS THERE LIFE ON EARTH?

to think they're spending
billions trying to find out
if there is life
on mars
hell, i spend
a few bucks a day
on gas
fighting the traffic
trying to make contact
with blank faces
once, at an intersection
i saw 2 cars collide
2 frustrated sticks of dynamite
explode
these dudes bursting
from their machines
throwing lefts & rights
they'd have killed
each other
if the cops
hadn't shown up

THE ONLY WAY

let's be simple now
simply gather up
our pain & stuff it
in a manila envelope
lick a couple of stamps
& mail it away
then let's close the curtains
lock the door
& tiptoe to the bedroom

in total silence
let's make love
it seems to be
the only way
to get by

LIFE IS A BALL

the next time
you're hassling with
your old man or old lady
making your car payments
working a 12 hour day or
trying to fix your car
consider this:
someday
your skin will wrinkle
your bones will ache
your eyes will dim
your strength will vanish
your mind will turn to jello
your liver will rot
your heart will stop
& the last thing
you'll probably do is
shit your pants

helluva reward, aint it?

JOHNNY McCOY (1946-63)

Alive he was a hero
but when he crashed his new vette
into the side
of the school bus garage
he became an instant legend
the next day
every punk in jr high
who fancied himself a "hood"
gathered at the scene
where a pimple faced sophomore
who claimed to have seen it
told us how McCoy
had been drag racing
on the school track &
had flown down the hill
at 90 mph
& then pointed to the spot
where the custodians
had peeled him off
the wall

FAMILY SNAPSHOT

my brother & i
would seem to have
everything going for us
since we are
reasonably intelligent
reasonably attractive
well-educated
& in xllnt health
but for
1 reason or another
we can't seem
to cut it
in this crazy deformed world
we can't seem
to hold down jobs
we are always bitching
about our circumstances &
we occasionally discuss
the merits of suicide

but

our sister is something else
she never ceases
to amaze us
she has been a diabetic
since birth

almost died at 3
has spent
the better part of her life
in doctors offices & hospitals
has had 3 or 4 miscarriages
her only kid die
after 2 days
& 1 by 1
the organs
thruout her body
deteriorate
the last we heard
she was slowly
going blind

yet

she is always laughing
always making jokes
about her problems
& is by far
the most optimistic
in the family

we know we have
a lot to learn
from her

THE HERO

i once dreamed that i was the hero
sitting in a motel room
puffing a marlboro
with a can of old milwaukee
resting on the windowsill
i was high on grass
& writing novels
in which i was the hero

RECIPE FOR WALKING TALL

cant remember
ever being too afraid
as kids
always seemed to know
how to deal with adversity
like the time
we were playing football
& someone kicked the ball
on old man myers lawn
& he charged out his front door
looking evil & sinister
& took it away
2 weeks later
halloween nite
we rounded up 50 kids
& surrounded his house
vinnie rang the doorbell
& when old myers answered
we pelted him with
150 raw eggs
cant remember him
ever taking away
our football
again
of course
this all happened
before we grew up
gained maturity
& were subtly beaten
into submission

FROM DEEP WITHIN A COFFIN

i died some time ago
though i'm not sure
exactly when it happened
looking back
it's pretty funny
to imagine how
i was walking
around & thinking
i was still alive

no funeral
no eulogy
no flowers
no tears
just a slow
painless death

i began noticing
little things like
not having a new idea
not meeting a new person
not having a new conversation
with an old friend
no trips
no adventures
& my girl started
talking about marriage

why not?
we've been living
together for a year
& watch a lotta tv
marriage seems like
a logical consequence
of death

& then there's
the people around me
no one has even
noticed i died
they keep talking
to me as if
i was alive

my advice
to anyone dying
is to maintain
a sense of humor
& an invincible
belief in reincarnation

I THINK I'LL GO TO THE NORTH POLE

not because I like cold weather
but because it's been
2 years now
since i quit
the road &
the bars
stopped changing
women & cities
like i do my socks
& i finally understand
what I miss about it

you see, i'm outa work
the bills are piling up
the refrigerator is empty
the car is falling apart
& suddenly i find
i have all these people
to answer to
like my worried wife
the landlord
dimwit personnel directors
& these new relatives i've acquired
who think i'm a creature
from Omecron 4

when i used to hitchhike
i always liked to do it alone
there was nothing worse
than standing in the rain
& having someone next to me
bitching & complaining
about standing in the rain

like i said, i'm not crazy
about cold weather
but at least at the North Pole
i could freeze to death
in peace &

solitude

SURVIVAL

it comes down
to a simple
math problem

(a child of 7 can figure it out)

take the number of times
they can knock you down
subtract the number of times
you can get back up

if the answer
is zero

you still have a chance

IT'S BEEN QUITE A YEAR

she claims to be psychic
insists she knows when things
are going to happen
last night she had a dream
about a red-headed comedian
who told a joke then asked
for the keys to my car

this morning i went out
to start the car & it was gone
the police tell me there's
little chance they'll ever
find it

HALLOWEEN 1976

little girl 8 yrs old removes
her minnie mouse mask
reaches into her bag of treats
grabs an apple takes a bite
the razor blade slashes
the inside of her mouth
she bleeds to death

MAYBE I'M BEING PETTY, BUT ...

All things considered
wasn't this supposed to be a partnership
like when you fall down
I pick you up & you do the same for me
it's like tag team wrestling
where I'm locked in battle
with Andre the Giant
he has me in a stranglehold
& you spring into action
jump into the ring & rip his ear off
instead I'm hanging from a cliff
by my fingertips
praying you'll reach out
& pull me to safety
but you keep stumbling around
always stepping on
my fingers

TODAY'S CHRISTOPHER COLUMBUS

Bravely sailing out
into a sea of discos
conquering new territories
where each terrain is different
the approach the same

When he finally reaches
the West Indies
he'll be damned
if he can remember
a single name

MR. ZUCCHINI

nothing he loves more
than going to parties
wearing just a long raincoat
which he opens & closes
all evening like some pervert
in a New York subway

last month
when the circus
came to town
he went out & bought
a pair of white leotards
painted his face red &
slipped into the center ring
wearing a blue shirt with
MR. ZUCCHINI printed on the back
he did a few cartwheels &
the crowd gave him
a big round of applause
thinking he was part
of the show

some people may think
there are too many nuts
running around these days
but I believe we could use
a few more

REST IN PEACE

Henri may not have been playing with a full deck, but he was a helluva nice guy. Henri died from watching TV. His favorite show was Marcus Welby.

After a while, he began to exist solely for Tuesday nights. He became so obsessed with the program that whenever a patient had a particular disease, so did Henri. One Tuesday, Henri had a heart attack. Another Tuesday, it was diabetes. He even caught VD once because someone on the show had it. Finally, one gloomy Tuesday night, a patient died

TODAY CATS, TOMORROW THE WORLD
(found poem)

The folks over at the American
Museum of Natural History
are busy maiming cats
to the tune of a half million
federal tax dollars
destroying the optic nerves
a portion of the inner ear &
the olfactory center of the brain
removing nerves in the male sex organs
surgically injuring sections of the brain
& then killing 'em after
electrical stimulation to the genitals
just to find out if
doing these things
affects the cats' sex lives
& now they're asking for
$200,000 more to continue
the experiments

I wonder who they'll work on
when they run out of
cats?

ADDING SALT TO THE WOUND

you wouldn't expect to find it here
not on this island paradise
a thousand miles from anywhere
yet here it was
I saw it right away
the pain
a dull distant gaze
etched in her eyes
4 days together
talking, drinking, hiking, swimming
she told me she hadn't had sex
in over a year
then on the third night
drinking retsina
she let loose
let it all out
like a wild animal
caged up too long
we fucked on the ground
on a pile of thorns & jagged rocks
both too drunk to know the difference
the next day our last together

we didn't speak of it
hiking miles away from everyone
lying nude together on the beach
turned on I reached for her
she didn't resist
just lay there motionless
her eyes wide open
with that same look of pain
as she took me in
rolling off I felt sick knowing
I had done something wrong
not sure what
but wishing I hadn't

SELLING PEANUTS

I stand on the grey corner
of a lifeless concrete city street
watching a man selling peanuts
and wonder my god
how can anyone survive
by selling peanuts
and then realize
I have nothing as valuable
as peanuts
to sell

LETTER TO THE REOCCURING
SOCIALIST PAPER IN MY MAILBOX

dear brothers & sisters
I don't know how
I got on your mailing list
but I would appreciate
being removed
on a scale of 1 to 10
I probably rank 8.3
on the insanity chart
so all I do now
is scribble poems &
pray for anarchy
I am tired
of the same old tired rhetoric
I believe it was bukowski who said politics
is like trying to fuck a cat in the ass
enuf said
carry on the struggle
but please leave me
to my beer & lowlife
power to the vegetables
right on!

SCORING

it's near closing time
10 minutes til 2
the bartender yells last call
you look to the end of the bar
to the only woman left
she's already said no
to 12 other guys
but you're drunk
so it doesn't matter
you pick up your beer
& wander down
you give it
your best shot
all the bullshit
you've been saving
for just this moment
she smiles
you know you're in
you're happy
she's happy
the night has not been wasted

THE SHAPE OF THINGS TO COME

good
god
the
weight
is
coming
down

good
solid
citizens
are
organizing
firing
squads

they
have
no
trouble
getting
volunteers

i
think
i'll
request
a
blindfold

THE CIRCLE GAME

you know it's a foolish game
but you seem to derive a perverse
satisfaction from playing
you are a prisoner
of some grand pleasure principle
so you continue to play
maybe you enjoy playing
because you are always
the one chosen to stand
in the middle of the circle
while the others join hands &
you search for the weakest link
a few days ago
you almost broke the circle
barreling your shoulder
into a 12 year old kid
who resembled sonny liston &
almost knocked him off his feet
but the kid was strong
held his ground & eventually caught
your chin with a clean uppercut

why you have not broken
the circle remains a mystery
you've seen others do it &
you know you are as capable
actually you have no idea
what you'll do if you manage
to break the circle
you've never seen the outside
you've heard rumors of its magnificence
you hope it's true
you'd hate to think
you've been wasting all your time
playing this foolish game

Greg Wyss

SOUR NOTES

I sit rocking in a frosty glass
an island with walls and moats
I just begged
a beautiful young girl with delicious skin
to leave me to my madness
so I can reflect upon others
that I've pleaded the same
I remember
walking the streets of Vienna
gliding thru the parks
listening to the orchestras
gazing up at St. Stephens
while my head played
in isolation alley

Mornings are center stage
to hate oneself
to ponder the heartless treatment
of those who come to give
evening will arrive
I will walk wrapped in a long blue coat
my collar concealing
my wretched face
a cigarette will dangle from my steel lips
my hair will fly as a bird
in the winds of winter

Venus will come
I will tie another knot
on my endless string
of stone emotion lovemaking
lost wives
will propagate in the night
lost loves
will spread their soft thighs
for others more capable of giving
I will remain a sad caricature
drink another ale and wonder
where I will be when I get old?

I GOT THEM DISHWASHING BLUES

all the time
we piss away
on chickenshit
stuff makes
my blood boil
take tonite
I'm washing dishes
& I figure
I have another
40 years left
which works out
to be 14,460 days
& if I wash dishes
twice a day
I'll only
have to do
this crap
29,220 more times

WHICH WAY TO THE MEN'S ROOM?

As I wander
from place to place
I am like a dog
frantically
in search of
a fire hydrant
frantically
in search of
that place
where I will
finally find
relief

WHAT DO I KNOW?

Rudy claims
to believe in
reincarnation
says he can
remember how
he last died
can picture it
as clear as
Rocky Mountain water
would have me
believe he was
in a foxhole
during WWII saw
a Japanese soldier
rushing toward him
with a bayonet
before the lights
went out
I have no reason
to doubt him

CRETE – JUNE 1973

the first thing you learn
on this simple island paradise
with its waters
as blue as its sky
is that it doesn't matter
what you look like
what you wear
how long your hair is
or where you're from
the people here don't care
just as long as you don't
fuck them over
they're strong
proud & independent
with 9 or 10 revolutions
in the past 150 years
the story going around is
last year a German tourist
was telling everyone
how much he loved this island
having been here
during the war
an old man
went into his house
grabbed his gun
& blew him away
seems his entire family
had been slaughtered
by the Germans
& he hadn't forgotten

THE BEAT GOES ON

Another bar
this time Houston
the creep
next to me
in his Johnny Miller
leisure suit
is telling anyone
who will listen
that you have to be
a self-starter
to make it in this
dog eat dog
world
I pray
someone
will drop
a quarter
In the jukebox
& scatter his words
like dust
Into oblivion

FATHER KNOWS BEST

my dad figures
by now
I should have
a comfortable desk
at IBM
2 cute kids
a mortgage &
all the other foundations
of the good life
but me
I'd rather be
far away
on a South Pacific island
eating fruit
surrounded by
succulent beauties
knowing I'll never
have to go back

TASTING THE 1970'S
3 EXCERPTS FROM THE NOVEL
WHEN LIFE WAS LIKE A CUCUMBER

Excerpt One

It was the strangest dream. I was standing in a Laundromat, folding my clothes, when suddenly out of nowhere Charles Darwin burst through the door. I knew immediately it was him when I saw the flowing white beard. He looked terrified.

"Quick, old chap!" he shouted, "I need to hide. They are right behind me."

No one had ever shouted at me before with an English accent. I didn't know what he was talking about, and as far as I could tell, he was alone.

"Who is right behind you?" I asked.

"I do not have time to explain," he bristled. "I need a place to hide."

If Charles Darwin needed a place to hide in order to survive, who was I to question him? After all, who knew more about survival than Charles Darwin? I had an idea. The dryer that I had just pulled my clothes out of was empty. I opened the glass door.

"Here," I said. "You can hide in the dryer."

Charles Darwin didn't hesitate. He took one giant step and leaped into the machine. He had been born way back in 1809, yet it was amazing how agile he was for his age. I closed the door. The dryer began to spin, and it suddenly occurred to me that I had pulled my clothes out before I used up all the minutes that I had paid for. I was about to open the door and rescue him when an angry mob of monkeys rushed into the Laundromat. There must have been nearly two dozen of them, each representing a different species. The largest one appeared to be the leader. Except for his hairy white belly, his fur was dark gray and was accented by two bands of color, one yellow and one black. His face was straight out of an Orange Sunshine acid trip. It had a red stripe down the middle and blue ridges on the sides. His lips and nostrils were red, and he was sporting a short yellow beard. I glanced down and saw that he had a humongous erection. The area around his genitals had taken the same LSD as his face, offering up a psychedelic display of reds, pinks, purples, and blues. This was one pissed-off monkey. He stared directly into my eyes, bobbed his head a few times, and then slapped the ground. He pressed his face against mine and introduced himself. His name was Mandrill, and his breath was horrible.

"Where the hell is Charles Darwin?" Mandrill screamed.

"I don't know," I said. "I haven't seen him. What do you want with him?"

"When we find the bastard," he answered, "we are going to kill him. We are going to stomp on his head and tear him apart, limb by limb."

"Why do you want to kill him?" I asked.

Mandrill raised his voice and slapped the ground again. I could tell that he was getting angrier.

"Are you kidding me?" he screeched. "The son of a bitch has given us a bad name. Have you ever read *On the Origin of Species*? He claims that humans are descended from us. For that insult, he deserves to die."

Mandrill turned to his fellow primates.

"Let's go," he said. "The asshole is not here."

The gang of monkeys quickly mobilized around Mandrill and then rushed out the door. I turned around and looked at the dryer. Charles Darwin was tumbling around in circles with his anxious face rubbing desperately against the glass. Poor Charlie looked more terrified than ever.

Photo by Ryan McGuire

Excerpt Two

And so began the Magical Mystery Tour.

It began at the only place it could. No words were necessary as the angel guided me into her bed and replenished me with the same raw passion and joy that she had blessed me with last summer. The evening turned into night and nourished me with all the mystery and excitement that blossoms whenever two bodies join together and are granted the freedom to explore each other for the first time. It took her nearly twenty-four hours to administer the cure. When she finished, I was once again ready to conquer the world. The celestial voices of John, Paul, George, and Ringo had created the soundtrack, but the angel was providing the transportation. It emerged in the form of a horse-drawn chariot encased inside an invisible bubble. Two white horses with bright-blue eyes stood side by side at the front of the gold carriage, ready to take us away. As the haunting sound of "All You Need Is Love" filled the room, the angel took my hand and whispered in my ear.

"I need to show you my new life," she said.

The white horses hustled the gold chariot out of the studio apartment and hauled us down five flights of stairs. We exited the building and came to an abrupt halt on the uneven sidewalk at the bottom of the steps. We were on East 7th Street, and it was a circus. Federico Fellini was in the middle of the road, directing traffic. Disheveled poets, struggling actors, aspiring filmmakers, and undiscovered musicians whirled past us in all directions. Lou Reed and Velvet Underground were standing on the corner, entertaining the mass of humanity with their favorite song "Rock & Roll." All five of the young dudes in Mott the Hoople were milling around on the opposite corner, smoking their cigarettes and waiting to go on next.

The chariot maneuvered its way through the poor and gritty neighborhoods, knocking over every metal garbage can that got in its way. It ventured north as far as Houston Street before turning right and making its way down to the East River. It raced along the shoreline until it reached the Manhattan Bridge and then made another sharp turn and galloped toward the Bowery. My head was spinning violently on my shoulders, trying to take it all in. I felt the angel squeeze my hand. Her warmth breath was in my ear.

"I want to take you to see the dancers," she said. "Then you will understand."

The white horses overheard her and changed directions. In a matter of seconds, the gold chariot found the nearest subway station. The earth opened its mouth and swallowed us up with one bite. As we raced through the dark bowels of Manhattan, I tried to read the seditious graffiti that ruled the subway walls and passing trains. The harrowing journey ended suddenly when, without warning, we were banished back to the earth's surface.

We stepped out of the chariot and entered a small theater.

"Where are we?" I asked.

"We are going to an off-Broadway show," the angel replied.

She pulled two tickets out of her back pocket. It was a tiny venue, and the theater was packed. There were two empty seats in the front row, just a few feet from the small stage. She had found us the two best seats in the house. We were barely seated when the lights went dim, the curtains went up, and the music started.

I didn't know anything about dance and I didn't recognize the music, but I was soon mesmerized by the grace and movements of the dancers. There were just two of them: one man and one woman. It was like watching poetry come to life. Barefoot and dressed in white almost see-through Greek tunics, they moved with a free-flowing spontaneity that revealed why she had brought me here.

The angel leaned over and asked me to watch how the two young artists personified a spiritual expression of the music that combined the purist elements of classical with the raw energy of rock 'n' roll. I liked the music, but I didn't understand what she was talking about. I nodded my head and pretended I did. She obviously knew more about modern dance than I did. As they glided across the stage, their arms were extended and fluid. They turned their knees out, thrust their hips forward, and stopped at the edge of the stage right in front of us. With one effortless motion, they opened and removed their tunics and tossed them on the floor. Celebrating their nudity, their firm and flawless bodies floated around the stage for several minutes as if they were being lifted into the air by both the wind and a surging sea. When the music reached its crescendo, the gifted dancers returned to the foot of the stage, faced the audience, and took a bow. I stood up and cheered. I was excited. The theater erupted into thunderous applause. I turned to the angel who was still in her seat.

"I understand," I shouted. "I understand."
Suddenly, I felt a hand on my shoulder...

Photo by Stefan Keller

Excerpt Three

When I came down, I was seated next to Jesus.

Owsley acid or not, I has to admit this was definitely one of the best hallucinogenic journeys that I had ever taken. I couldn't prove it, but it may have been the only time in human history that an LSD trip had turned into an actual real-life trip. I was staring out the window into the darkness of the Atlantic Ocean thirty thousand feet below me. The moon had formed a perfect circle, a lightbulb frozen in suspended animation. A baby was crying. I was trapped inside the stomach of a gigantic bird, surrounded by comatose bodies lined up six abreast as it hurled its passengers through an endless black tunnel. I was confident that I could handle anything now, considering where I had been over the past twelve hours. Still, I couldn't believe my eyes when I saw who was sitting next to me.

"Are you all right?" he asked.

I had to think about it before I responded. I was having trouble remembering how I got here. Before I could answer, Jesus reached out to shake my hand.

"Hi," he said, "my name is Tony."

His disguise was a good one. Wearing faded blue jeans and a brown and rust-colored parka over a dark-blue T-shirt, he easily passed for just another hippie. His accent only added to his ruse.

It sounded English, but it was slightly different. The accent and calling himself Tony made for a good cover, but he wasn't fooling me. I recognized him immediately. I had seen him in countless pictures since I was a child: in church, in books and magazines, and in black frames on the kitchen walls in the homes of my Catholic friends. His long brown hair was unmistakable. Shoulder-length and wavy, it gave off a glow that served to accentuate his closely trimmed mustache and beard. His baby-blue eyes were kind, and he possessed a gentle smile. If Jesus wished to remain incognito to the other passengers, I wasn't going to be the one to blow his cover. I played along.

"Hi, I'm Jeff," I said, exchanging the pleasantry and shaking his hand.

"Seriously," he insisted, "are you all right?"

I must have looked pretty bad for Jesus to be so concerned. Should I tell him my story? I was on my second day without sleep, had just come down from an acid trip, and was on an Air Bahamas flight to Luxembourg. I didn't even know where Luxembourg was. If I couldn't tell my tale to Jesus, whom could I tell it to?

Jesus was easy to talk to. He listened patiently while I spilled my guts. He chuckled when I told him about purchasing my ticket on LSD and complimented me on the skill I had displayed by actually making it to the airport and solving the riddle of checking in and boarding an airplane. He looked a little worried when I confessed that I had never heard of Luxembourg, admitted that I wasn't sure where it was, and revealed that I had no idea what I was going to do when I got there. He pondered my dilemma for a moment and then calmly reached out for my hand. His voice was sincere.

"You need to go to Amsterdam first," he said.

When I explained that I didn't know where that was or how to get there, he told me not to worry. He promised to help me when we landed in Luxembourg. My curiosity was getting the best of me. What was Jesus doing on an airplane? Why was he flying to Europe and going to Luxembourg of all places? Why was he pretending his name was Tony? Finally, summoning up the courage to question him, I asked Jesus what he was doing here.

I had to concede it was a convincing story. He continued to pretend his name was Tony, and he claimed to be from Australia. He said that he had been in South America for the last two years, living mostly in Peru. When I asked him if people recognized him there, he smiled.

"Only the children," he said softly.

He told me how they would often rush up to him on the streets whenever he walked alone. They were usually in small groups, and they always shouted the same words at him as they tugged at his arms and pulled on his shirt.

He laughed. "It was always Hay-zeus Kris-toes, Hay-zeus Kris-toes," he said.

"What did you do?" I asked.

"Oh, nothing much," he said. "They always asked for money, so I would give each of them a small coin. That seemed to satisfy them. They would take my coins, giggle, and run away."

"Wasn't that a hassle?"

"Not really," he said with a wink. "It was my cross to bear, if you know what I mean."

I could relax now. He knew that I knew. No more subterfuge. Now that I shared the secret of his real identity, I could sit back and enjoy the flight. I don't know why, but Jesus was easing me into my new life. I wasn't worried anymore. A thousand pounds had been lifted off my shoulders. Everything would be cool. I had left the US, and I would soon be in Europe.

I must have fallen asleep because the next thing I remember, Jesus was tapping me gently on my shoulder.

"We've landed," he said. "It's time to get off the plane."

We were seated near the back of the plane, so we were among the last ones off. I followed Jesus into the terminal and through the narrow hallways to the baggage claim area. I was relieved to find that my backpack had also made it across the Atlantic. Jesus remained true to his word. After we both retrieved our backpacks, he stayed by my side and guided me through the passport control process. I was completely disoriented. The brief one or two hours of sleep that I managed to catch before we landed had left me in worse shape than if I had not slept at all. Jesus went first and sailed right through. He had his passport stamped and then waited for me on the other side. He had probably done this several thousand times before. I wondered how many passports he had amassed over the years and how he had managed to score one from Australia of all places. I was a little nervous when it was my turn, but I was worrying over nothing. The passport dude asked me a couple of questions in English, stamped my passport, and welcomed me to Luxembourg. I was officially in Europe.

The airport was only about five miles from the center of Luxembourg City where Jesus said that I could purchase a ticket to Amsterdam. I was already freaking out about the money exchange thing. Jesus laughed. He told me that I didn't need to be converting my traveler's checks into anything right now. He explained that Luxembourg and Belgian francs were interchangeable but said that I didn't need to purchase either of them. He said that I should wait until I got to Amsterdam and then get some Dutch guilders. He reached into his front pocket and pulled out some funny-looking money.

"Let me buy your ticket for you," he offered. "I'll show you how to do it."

Jesus handed me a train schedule and

showed me how to read it. First, we would take the short train ride into the city to the central train station. There we would purchase my ticket to Amsterdam. As we rode into the city, Jesus went over the schedule with me several times. He wanted to make sure that I understood that I would be changing trains a couple of times while traveling through Belgium to get to the Dutch city of Maastricht. Once there, I would change trains one last time to complete the final leg of my journey.

I stood next to Jesus at the ticket counter and watched him procure my ticket. He then walked me over to the platform where my train was scheduled to depart.

"You are on your own now," he said. "Good luck to you."

"Thank you, Jesus," I said. "I'll never forget what you did for me."

Jesus smiled and placed a hand on each of my shoulders.

"It's Tony," he said. "Remember that my name is Tony when you tell this story."

"I will," I said. "Your secret is safe with me."

Greg Wyss

As part of a generation shaped by the Vietnam War, drug culture and sexual revolution, beloved author, poet and entrepreneur Greg Wyss was well known in the small press world of the 1970's. His poems and stories appeared in dozens of literary publications. A collection of his classic work *Sit Down And Have A Beer* was published in 1977 by Realities Library in San Diego, California.

A graduate of Northeastern University, Greg retired in 2015 to resume his writing career after the wireless communications company he co-founded was purchased by a competitor. Greg and his wife Barbara live in Houston, Texas.

Greg's first novel, When Life Was Like A Cucumber, was published in 2019 and can be purchased by visiting www.gregwyss.com

Made in the USA
Monee, IL
17 July 2022